Clip-Art Features for Church Newsletters 5

Illustrations for Bulletin Boards,
Home Bulletins, and News Releases

Clip-Art Features for Church Newsletters 5

George W. Knight, Compiler
Howard Paris, Illustrator

BAKER BOOK HOUSE
Grand Rapids, Michigan 49516

Contents

1

Church Support

God's Love for the Church

What would happen if the church were taken from your life? Would it really make a difference? What would change, if anything? The answer depends on how committed you are and the value you place on the church. We as Christians must remember that the worth of the church is based on God's assessment of its value and not on ours. What is of great worth to God must also hold great worth for us.

How valuable is the church to God? It cost him his only Son. He purchased the church with the the shed blood of Jesus Christ. Since God loves the church this much, none of us dares treat it with indifference.

Please Do Not Feed the Animals!

Some church members are as stubborn as a mule about doing church work but as sly as a fox in their own business deals. Others are as busy as a bee in spreading the latest gossip but as quiet as a mouse in spreading the gospel of Christ.

Some Christians are as eager as a beaver about a barbecue or a church supper but as lazy as a dog when it comes to prayer meeting or teaching a class. Stop acting like one of these animals about your church and get involved in its ministry!

First Impressions *Are* Important

The first seven seconds are of crucial importance in our encounters with each other. In those few seconds we make up our minds about the persons we meet and they make up their minds about us. Social researchers believe it takes only seven seconds for a salesman to judge a customer; seven seconds for a mugger to size up a potential victim; seven seconds to sense attraction for a member of the opposite sex. This rapid analysis and reaction is what we call a "first impression."

If it takes just seven seconds to make up our minds about another person, how long does it take visitors to make up their minds about our church? Not long. This means we should take every opportunity to greet visitors and make them feel welcome as soon as they arrive. Remember, we never get a second chance to make a first impression.

Many Streams Make a Mississippi

The Mississippi River is only a few feet wide at the place where it begins. But only thirty miles further downstream, it swells to a width of fifty feet. Numerous streams flow into the Mississippi along its entire length until it becomes the largest river in North America. The mighty Mississippi would not exist without the contribution of these smaller streams.

This says a great deal about what it takes to make a great church. A few people can't do it in their own strength. It takes all of us working together, using our gifts and talents in the kingdom cause, to keep our church healthy and strong.

The Weight of a Snowflake

A squirrel once asked a bird to tell him how much a snowflake weighed.

"Why, a snowflake doesn't weigh anything," the bird replied. Then the squirrel told this story.

"I was sitting in a tree when it began to snow," he said. "Just for fun, I counted the snowflakes as they settled on the twigs and needles of a single branch. The number reached exactly 6,834. When the next snowflake fell—the next weightless snowflake, as you say—the branch broke off."

The bird thought about this for a minute. "If something as light as a single snowflake can snap a twig," he declared, "perhaps the combined weight of people working together in a church can also make a difference."

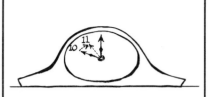

The Power of a Single Hour

A cartoon pictured two stone masons, trowels in hand, standing in front of a huge, ornate tower. One said to the other, "I skimped a little on the foundation, but no one will ever know." Closer examination of the tower shows that it is the Tower of Pisa, now known as the Leaning Tower of Pisa because of the shifting of its foundation several years after its construction.

This cartoon declares dramatically that *little things make a lot of difference.* Consider a single hour, for example. It's a small thing—one of 168 in a week. But if you spend that one hour each week in Sunday school, it will make a difference in your life.

When people gather for Sunday school, they are declaring, "I need to hear what God's Word says, and I need the fellowship of other believers." Join others for a great hour of Bible study this week. See you in Sunday school.

2

Discipleship and Christian Influence

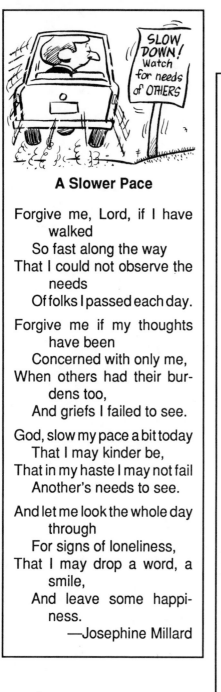

A Slower Pace

Forgive me, Lord, if I have
walked
    So fast along the way
That I could not observe the
needs
    Of folks I passed each day.

Forgive me if my thoughts
have been
    Concerned with only me,
When others had their bur-
dens too,
    And griefs I failed to see.

God, slow my pace a bit today
    That I may kinder be,
That in my haste I may not fail
    Another's needs to see.

And let me look the whole day
through
    For signs of loneliness,
That I may drop a word, a
smile,
    And leave some happi-
ness.
          —Josephine Millard

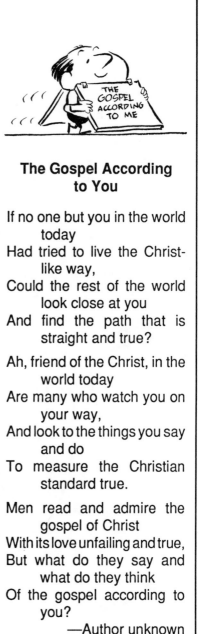

The Gospel According to You

If no one but you in the world
today
Had tried to live the Christ-
like way,
Could the rest of the world
look close at you
And find the path that is
straight and true?

Ah, friend of the Christ, in the
world today
Are many who watch you on
your way,
And look to the things you say
and do
To measure the Christian
standard true.

Men read and admire the
gospel of Christ
With its love unfailing and true,
But what do they say and
what do they think
Of the gospel according to
you?
          —Author unknown

YOUR TEST PAPER

Tests for a Christian

The weather test: Are you a sailboat Christian—making progress in the Lord if the winds are favorable? Or are you a tugboat Christian—plowing right ahead even though the gales are against you?

The worldliness test: Do you think as the world thinks, go where the world goes, act as the world acts? Does your life give evidence of having your affections set on things above, not on things on the earth?

The work test: How much of your energy is being given to the work of the Lord? Is it a reasonable portion of your total energies?

The witness test: Are you commending Christ to those who do not know him as Savior and Lord by the way you live as well as through your spoken words?

More Shine and Less Talk

I would not give anything for your profession of faith unless it can be seen. Lamps do not talk; they shine. A lighthouse sounds no drums; it beats no gong; and yet its guiding beams are seen by imperiled mariners.

—C. H. Spurgeon

Authentic Doctrine

The words we speak, the songs we sing,
The doctrines that we teach
Will have their greatest meaning
When we practice what we preach.

—Author unknown

Puzzling People

Angels from their realms on high
Look down on us with wondering eye—
That where we are but passing guests,
We build such strong and solid nests;
But where we hope to dwell for aye,
We scarce take heed one stone to lay.

—Author unknown

Unless

All the water in the world,
  However hard it tried,
Could never sink a sailing ship
  Unless it got inside.

All the evil in the world—
  The wickedness and sin—
Can never sink your soul's
  fair craft
Unless you let it in.
                    —Author unknown

Doing God's Will

To *know* the will of God,
  This is the greatest knowledge.

To *find* the will of God,
  This is the greatest discovery.

To *do* the will of God,
  This is the greatest achievement.

3

Evangelism and Visitation

Visitation's Accomplishments

V italizes the work of the church.

I increases enrollment.

S ecures cooperation between church and home.

I nspires regular attendance.

T ypifies the spirit of Christ.

A ffords soul-winning opportunities.

T ouches the person far away from Christ.

I nsures your own spiritual growth.

O beys the command of Christ.

N urtures friendships with new people.

When Do We Need Revival?

It is very evident that we need revival:

—When it is easier to work than to worship.

—When it is easier to read a novel than the Bible.

—When it is easier to support the club than the church.

—When it is easier to condemn people than to pray for their salvation.

—When it is easier to hold grudges than to forgive.

The Soul-Winner's Prayer

Oh, give me, Lord, thy love for souls,
  For lost and wandering sheep,
That I may see the multitudes
  And weep as thou dost weep.

Help me to see the tragic plight
  Of souls far off in sin;
Help me to love, to pray, and go
  To bring the wandering in.
      —Eugene M. Harrison

The Power of the "V" Word

The key to reaching people for Christ is a single word which has often been referred to as the "V" word.

It is call the "V" word because it is so Very important. It takes Valor and Vigor to make it work. But it will help us out of the Valley. It will bring in a Variety of people who need Jesus. It will make us a people with a Vision. It is Vital to the growth of our church. To accomplish this work, we must have Volunteers—people who will Vow to carry it through.

What is this "V" word? Visitation, of course!

Our Christian Responsibility

We are found, to find another.
We are told, to tell another.
We are won, to win another.
We are saved, to save another.

Asking Power

A famous American businessman bought a large insurance policy on himself. It was so large that the newspapers carried the story. One of the businessman's friends, an insurance agent, asked why he didn't buy the policy from him since he was a personal friend. The businessman replied, "You never asked me."

Could it be that some of our neighbors would attend church services or Sunday school if we just asked them? Is it possible that someone will never accept Christ because we never asked them? Be sure to take time to tell others the good news of Jesus and his salvation.

4

Inspiration

Trust for the Journey

I do not know what still awaits,
　Or what the morrow brings;
But with the glad salute of
　faith,
　I hail its opening wings!

For this I know that in my Lord
　Shall all my needs be met;
And I can trust the heart of
　him
　Who has not failed me yet.
　　　　　—Author unknown

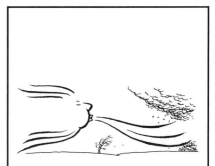

The Winds of Renewal

The strong, blustery winds of winter are hard to endure, but let's think of these winds as indicators of the approaching spring and forces for God's renewing work in our lives.

Let the winter wind blow away the physical sickness from your life, along with the winter blahs, depression, and lethargy. Let the wind of the Spirit lift weight of sin and release you to a new peace and joy.

Blow, winter wind. Push the storm clouds away. Bring in spring—the reminder of the resurrection, and God's renewing work in our lives.

I Saw God This Morning

I saw God this morning,
    Just past the break of day,
When the sun came over the
        mountainside
    And pushed the fog away.

The mighty oak that towered
        high
    Above the other trees
Spoke as it stood so straight
        and tall
    Of the God who stands by
    me.

The tender touch of the gentle
        breeze
    That whispered through
    the air
Seemed to speak of God's
        great love
    That is found at a place of
        prayer.

Yes, I saw God in everything
    As I sat beside the brook,
And looked at things that he
        has made
    And read his blessed book.
            —Hiram A. LeMay

What to Pray For

Do not pray for an easy life; pray to be a stronger person. Do not pray for tasks equal to your powers; pray for powers equal to your tasks. Then the doing of your work shall be no miracle, but *you* will be the miracle.

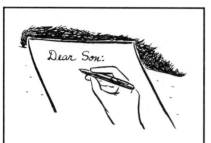

Dear Son: This Is How Much I Loved You

I loved you enough to ask where you were going, with whom, and what time you would be home.

I loved you enough to insist that you clean your room—a job that would have taken me just a few minutes but a chore you sometimes stretched into a couple of hours.

I loved you enough to let you see my anger, disappointment, and tears. Children must learn that their parents are not perfect.

I loved you enough to let you take responsibility for your actions, even when the penalties were harsh.

But most of all, I loved you enough to say "No." Someday, when you have children of your own, you will understand the value and necessity of this two-letter word.

Lend a Helping Hand

If you cannot write a volume,
    If you cannot write a song,
Maybe you can help some person
    Who has suffered some great wrong.

For it doesn't take a fortune
    Nor sermon great and grand
Just to show a little kindness
    Or to lend a helping hand.

Think it over, friend and neighbor,
    Were you in this person's place,
How a little bit of sunshine
    From a kind and smiling face
Might uplift you on your journey
    As you travel through the land.
Therefore, pray and God will show you
    How to lend a helping hand.
        —Walter E. Isenhour

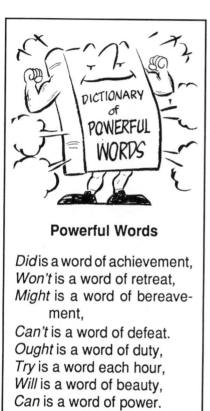

Powerful Words

Did is a word of achievement,
Won't is a word of retreat,
Might is a word of bereave-
ment,
Can't is a word of defeat.
Ought is a word of duty,
Try is a word each hour,
Will is a word of beauty,
Can is a word of power.
—Author unknown

Work that Lasts

If you want something to last
a season, plant flowers.
If you want something to last
a lifetime, plant trees.
If you want something to last
an eternity, plant
churches.
—Mark Platt

The Gift of Friendship

True friendship is indeed a
gift,
A treasure from above;
For friendship's just another
part
Of God's great gift of love.
—Author unknown

My Guidebook

There is a book more precious
    Than anything on earth;
No wealth of gold or jewels
    Can equal it in worth.

I go to it in trouble,
    And though my heart is
    sore,
It always gives me comfort—
    I love it more and more.

When doubtful what is best
    for me,
    I seek its guidance true;
And if I search with open mind,
    It tells me what to do.
          —Author unknown

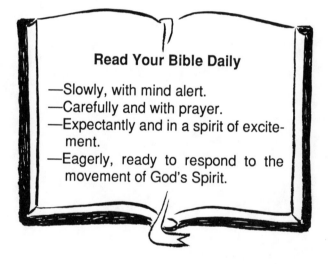

Read Your Bible Daily

—Slowly, with mind alert.
—Carefully and with prayer.
—Expectantly and in a spirit of excitement.
—Eagerly, ready to respond to the movement of God's Spirit.

How to Beat the Summer Heat

—Refresh your mind by reading the Bible.
—Face the billowy breeze of the Holy Spirit.
—Shower yourself with God's bountiful blessings.
—Drink from the springs of living water that will quench your thirst forever.
—Break the ice with someone against whom you are holding a grudge.
—Create a pleasant climate in your home where joy can grow.

No Time-Outs

In a football or basketball game the coach often calls a time-out to give the team a chance to set up a crucial play. But life does not work this way. We can't stop the clock to think about our problems. We cannot save, store, or stretch time. Time moves on, minute by minute and hour by hour, whether we waste it or use it wisely.

Time spent in the service of our Lord and his church is time well spent. Let's make sure we invest a portion of our time in the work of God's kingdom.

Walking with God

Sometimes I walk in the
    shadow,
    Sometimes in sunlight
    clear;
But whether in gloom or
    brightness
    The Lord is very near.

Sometimes I walk in the
    valley,
    Sometimes on the moun-
    tain crest,
But whether on low or high
    land,
    The Lord is manifest.

Sometimes I walk in green
    pastures,
    Sometimes on barren land;
But whether in peace or
    danger
    The Lord is close at hand.
        —Author unknown

Don't Miss the Music

A master organist whose fingers grew too old to play was made custodian of the organ in a famous cathedral. One day a visitor came to the cathedral and asked to play the organ, but the custodian refused.

The visitor persisted until he was finally given permission to play a few notes. He filled the cathedral with such beautiful music that the old organist was entranced. He asked the visitor his name, and he replied, "My name is Felix Mendelssohn."

Until the end of his life, the old organist told this story to everyone he met. "To think," he would exclaim, "that I almost missed hearing Mendelssohn play!"

How many people have been the losers for not letting the Master touch their hearts with heavenly music! Don't miss the music of the Savior's love in your life.

Assure Your Children of Your Love

A study of high schoolers shows how important it is to tell our children we love them. After the counselors had worked long enough to establish a good relationship with ten students who were having problems, they asked them how long it had been since their parents had told them they loved them. Not a single one could remember having heard such a comment.

By contrast, ten of the best-adjusted teens answered the question by saying "this morning" or "last night," or indicated they had been verbally assured of their parents' love within the last few hours.

5

Jesus Christ

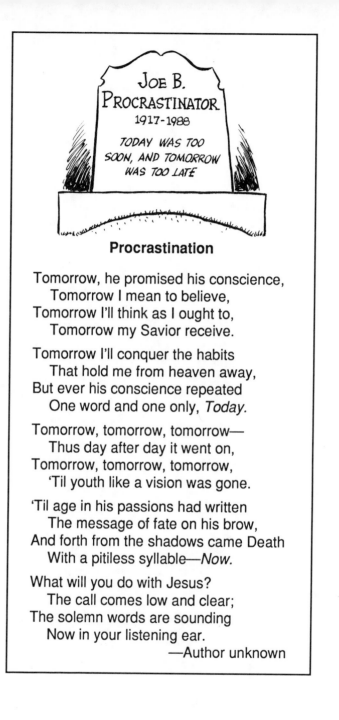

JOE B.
PROCRASTINATOR
1917-1988

TODAY WAS TOO
SOON, AND TOMORROW
WAS TOO LATE

Procrastination

Tomorrow, he promised his conscience,
   Tomorrow I mean to believe,
Tomorrow I'll think as I ought to,
   Tomorrow my Savior receive.

Tomorrow I'll conquer the habits
   That hold me from heaven away,
But ever his conscience repeated
   One word and one only, *Today*.

Tomorrow, tomorrow, tomorrow—
   Thus day after day it went on,
Tomorrow, tomorrow, tomorrow,
   'Til youth like a vision was gone.

'Til age in his passions had written
   The message of fate on his brow,
And forth from the shadows came Death
   With a pitiless syllable—*Now*.

What will you do with Jesus?
   The call comes low and clear;
The solemn words are sounding
   Now in your listening ear.
                  —Author unknown

Easter's Victory Message

Easter points to one great event—the resurrection of Jesus Christ. Easter was God's final stamp of approval on our Lord's life. Jesus had endured anguish, agony, and death in the belief that God would not remain silent in the face of such injustice. Everything Jesus had taught about the real meaning of life was proven when God raised him from the dead.

The resurrection of Jesus speaks a victorious word to us today. Easter affirms the truth that God lives in us and we in him. May this Easter vision give us strength for victorious living as we proclaim the living Christ to others.

Hands for Christ

During World War II, a church in a French village was destroyed. Underneath the rubble workers found a statue of Christ, unbroken except for the two hands, which were missing.

In time the church was rebuilt. A sculptor offered to rebuild the hands on the statue before it was placed in the churchyard. But the church members replied, "We will put it up without the hands. This will be a reminder to us that Christ has no hands but our hands with which to minister to human need."

A Resource for Problem Solving

Problems! Everyone has one or two. There is no pill that we can take to ward off problems. And the person who says he never has any is either deluding himself or misrepresenting the truth.

Just think of the time and energy you spend trying to solve problems. Some are easily solved, but others demand a lot of effort.

To be successful in life, you have to become a problem solver. This requires discipline and hard work. The easiest course is to ignore problems, but this usually causes even bigger problems further down the line.

The main difference between problems for the Christian and the non-Christian is that we have a resource for problem solving in the person of Jesus Christ. He promises to be with us and to help us in the struggle. Call on him often as your problem-solving partner!

6

Prayer

Prayer Does Change Things

Prayer changes situations and circumstances. Abraham prayed, and God gave him a son. Jacob prayed, and he was reconciled with his brother Esau. Paul and Silas prayed, and the prison was shaken open and the hardened jailor was saved.

Prayer changes the person who prays. David prayed, and he became a man after God's own heart. Peter prayed, and he became the Lord's chief apostle.

Prayer changes our perspective. Prayer permits us to view the things of this life from the perspective of the Lord of the universe. We are led by the Spirit of God through prayer to view ourselves and others from God's point of view.

Too Busy to Pray?

Forgive me, Lord, that I allow
My days and hours to be
So filled with trifling tasks, that oft
I find no time for thee.

My thoughts too oft are occupied
With countless earthly things,
When thou wouldst have them mount on high
By faith with eagle wings.

Too busy; O forgive, dear Lord,
That I should ever be
Too much engrossed in worldly tasks
To spend an hour with thee.
—A. B. Christiansen

A Prayer for Everyone

Lord, when we are wrong, make us willing to change. And when we are right, make us easy to live with.

—Peter Marshall

What a Day!

I overslept; I burned the toast;
  The bus left me again;
I flunked the test; my ink pen clogged;
  I've got a stomach pain.

The car just quit; my date is sick;
  The dog just ate my food;
I try to cope—it's not that bad—
  Except my attitude.

The only way, it seems to me,
  To make it through the day
Is when I stop, to call time-out,
  And take the time to pray.

—Author unknown

7

Seasonal and Christian Year

Recipe for a Happy New Year

Take twelve months. Clean them thoroughly of all bitterness, hate, and jealousy. Then arrange each month into 28, 30, or 31 different parts, but don't make up the whole batch at once. Prepare it one day at a time out of these ingredients.

Mix well into each day one part each of faith, patience, courage, work, hope, faithfulness, generosity, and kindness. Blend this mixture with a pint of prayer. Season the whole with a dash of good spirits, a sprinkle of fun, a pinch of play, and a cupful of good humor.

Pour this batter into a vessel of love and cook thoroughly over radiant joy. When done, serve the day with a smile in the name of your Savior, who fills the new year with love and joy.

A Prayer for the New Year

A whole new year is mine today;
May I be wiser, Lord, I pray—
To strengthen friendships old and true
And learn to cherish new ones, too—
To keep on learning and to grow
A little deeper as I go.

To cast aside each grudge and grief,
And hold fast to a firm belief
That life is joyous, gracious, good,
When lived in terms of brotherhood.

—Author unknown

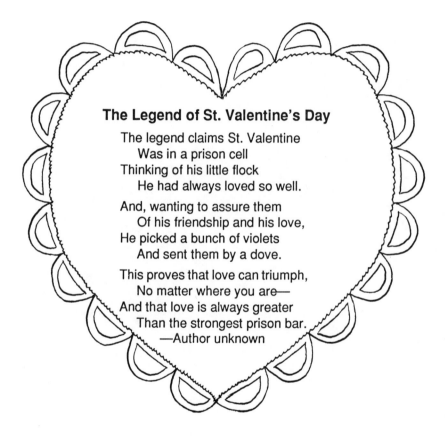

The Legend of St. Valentine's Day

The legend claims St. Valentine
    Was in a prison cell
Thinking of his little flock
    He had always loved so well.

And, wanting to assure them
    Of his friendship and his love,
He picked a bunch of violets
    And sent them by a dove.

This proves that love can triumph,
    No matter where you are—
And that love is always greater
    Than the strongest prison bar.
        —Author unknown

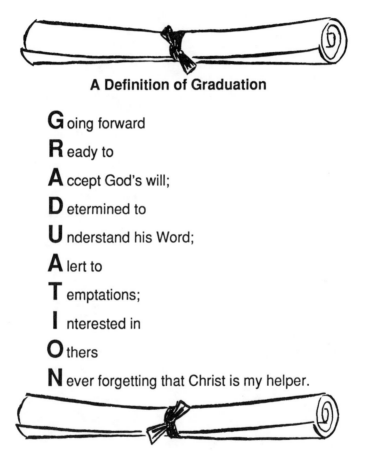

A Definition of Graduation

G oing forward

R eady to

A ccept God's will;

D etermined to

U nderstand his Word;

A lert to

T emptations;

I nterested in

O thers

N ever forgetting that Christ is my helper.

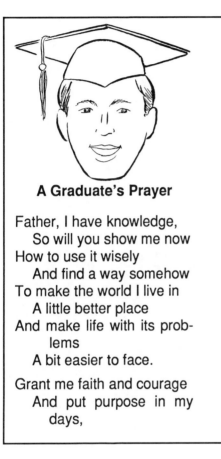

A Graduate's Prayer

Father, I have knowledge,
    So will you show me now
How to use it wisely
    And find a way somehow
To make the world I live in
    A little better place
And make life with its prob-
    lems
    A bit easier to face.

Grant me faith and courage
    And put purpose in my
    days,
And show me how to serve
    you
    In the most effective ways
So all my education,
    My knowledge and my skill,
May find their true fulfillment
    As I learn to do your will.

And may I ever be aware
    In everything I do
That knowledge comes from
    learning,
    And wisdom comes from
    you.
                    —Author unknown

A Mother's Creation

You painted no madonnas
    On chapel walls in Rome,
But with a touch more
    precious
    You lived one in your home.

You wrote no lofty poems
    That critics counted art,
But with a nobler vision
    You lived them in your
    heart.

You carved no shapeless
    marble
    Into a great design,
But with a finer sculpture
    You shaped this soul of
    mine.
                —Author unknown

A Mother's Prayer

I wash the dirt from little feet
    And as I wash I pray,
"Lord, keep them ever pure
    and true
    To walk the narrow way."

I wash the grime from little
    hands
    And earnestly I ask,
"Lord, may they ever yielded
    be
    To do the humblest task."

I scrub the clothes they soil so
    soon
    And pray, "Lord, may their
    dress
Throughout eternal ages be
    Your robe of righteous-
    ness."
                —Author unknown

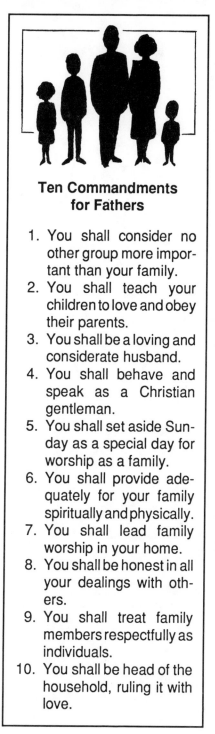

Ten Commandments for Fathers

1. You shall consider no other group more important than your family.
2. You shall teach your children to love and obey their parents.
3. You shall be a loving and considerate husband.
4. You shall behave and speak as a Christian gentleman.
5. You shall set aside Sunday as a special day for worship as a family.
6. You shall provide adequately for your family spiritually and physically.
7. You shall lead family worship in your home.
8. You shall be honest in all your dealings with others.
9. You shall treat family members respectfully as individuals.
10. You shall be head of the household, ruling it with love.

Fathers on the Job

As long as there are fathers who
Turn homeward when the day is through
With buoyant steps and smiling face,
Whose pride is in a simple place;
Who live and love and serve the Lord;
Who seek no tribute or reward
Except the privilege to be
Head of a Christian family;
We need not fear—for just this long
Our homes are safe, our land is strong!

—Author unknown

A Father's Example

There are little eyes upon you,
  And they're watching night
    and day;
There are little ears that listen
  To every word you say.

There are little hands all eager
  To do the things you do;
And a little boy who's dream-
    ing
  Of the day he'll be like you.

You're the little fellow's idol,
  You're the wisest of the
    wise;
In his little mind, about you
  No suspicions ever rise.

He believes in you devoutly,
  Holds that all you say and
    do
He will say and do it your way
  When he's grown up just
    like you.

You are setting an example
  Every day in all you do
For the little boy who's wait-
    ing
  To grow up to be like you.
      —Edgar A. Guest

A Mother's Thanksgiving Prayer

Lord, thank you for this sink of dirty dishes; we have good food to eat.

Thank you for this big pile of dirty clothes; there's no doubt that we have plenty of things to wear!

Thank you for these unmade beds; they were clean and comfortable last night.

Thank you for this finger-smudged refrigerator; it has served us faithfully for a long time.

Thank you for the tall grass that needs mowing; we enjoy our spacious yard.

Thank you for that slamming door; the children are healthy and able to run and play.

A Thanksgiving Prayer

O thou Creator of all things, we lift up our hearts in gratitude for this day's happiness—

For the mere joy of living;
For the sweet peace of the country and the
    pleasant bustle of the town;
For all things bright and beautiful;
For friendship and good company;
For a time to play when the day's work is done
    and for health and a glad heart to enjoy it.

And above all, we thank thee for the sure hope and promise of an endless life which thou hast given us in Jesus Christ, our Lord. Amen.

—John Baillie

A Christmas Prayer

A day that's full of happiness
    For you and yours we pray,
And may a gleam of friendly cheer
    Melt all your cares away.

Let Christ abide within your heart
    And hallow all your home;
And may you say with Tiny Tim,
    "God bless us everyone."
                 —Author unknown

Some Definitions of Christmas

Christmas is the light that burns eternally in the hearts of people wherever the message of "Peace on earth to men of goodwill" is believed.

Christmas is peace in a world where people have been alienated from each other by hatred and jealousy.

Christmas is love that flows from one heart to another.

Christmas is giving to those who cannot give to us. It is visiting the neglected, lifting the fallen, giving hope to the hopeless, living the spirit of goodwill to others.

Christmas is surrender of our lives to Christ in renewed dedication, making him Lord of our lives.

A Christmas Prayer

May the Christ of whom the angels sang in that first Christmas chorus bring peace to your hearts at this Christmas season. May the "joy of heaven to earth come down" bring each of you abundant joy and blessing throughout each day of the new year as you crown him King in your hearts. Through Jesus Christ our Lord. Amen.

Make Room for Christmas

Let not our hearts be busy
inns
That have no room for thee,
But cradles of the living Christ
And his nativity.
—Author unknown

Christmas Meets Our Greatest Need

If our greatest need had been information,
God would have sent us an educator.

If our greatest need had been technology,
God would have sent us a scientist.

If our greatest need had been money,
God would have sent us an economist.

If our greatest need had been pleasure,
God would have sent us an entertainer.

But our greatest need was forgiveness—
So God sent us a Savior.

8

Sentence Sermons

The Vital Difference

Love makes a way, while indifference finds an excuse.

A Matter of Perspective

Don't worry about getting old. It is better to be "over the hill" than under it.

Living Proof

It is good to be a Christian and know it; it is even better to be a Christian and *show* it.

An Easy Choice

The trouble with most of us is that we had rather be ruined by praise than saved by criticism.

How to Save Face

The best way to "save face" is to keep the bottom half shut.

Careful Study Essential

Don't study the Bible "hit and miss"; you'll miss more than you hit.

A Majority of One

One person with conviction is worth more than 99 with opinions.

Don't Compare

You cannot become a saint by comparing yourself to a sinner.

A Losing Proposition

The trouble with being a good sport is that you have to lose to prove you are.

A Rx That Doesn't Work

No matter how long you nurse a grudge, it won't get better.

Real Expense

If you think education is expensive, try ignorance!

Worry Defined

Worry is the senseless process of using today to clutter up tomorrow's opportunities with leftover problems from yesterday.